Drillers Offsider

EVERYTHING You Need to Know About Being an RC or Diamond Drillers Assistant And Progressing to Driller

1st Edition

By Johnny Bevan

for any reparation, damages, or monetary loss due to the information herein, either directly or indirectly.

Respective authors own all copyrights not held by the publisher.

The information herein is offered for informational purposes solely, and is universal as so. The presentation of the information is without contract or any type of guarantee assurance.

Table of Contents

Introduction

This book explains the drillers' offsider's job description – the usual daily tasks, lifestyle, and routine. It gives samples of how a typical day goes for someone with this position.

The job as a drillers offsider is challenging, but it pays well. It is not suited for the faint heart. If you want to become one, you have to prepare all aspects of your life, especially the physical, mental, and emotional parts.

No matter how prepared you are, the job offer will not come on a silver platter. You will need to extend effort and spend money while looking for a job. This book has a dedicated chapter on how to become more "sellable" to probable employers. Like in any kinds of jobs, you will stand out among the hoards of competition if you have related experience in similar industries. You will find in this book helpful tips on what other jobs you can apply to learn the skills and gain experience you can use when applying as a drillers offsider.

This book also makes it easier for you to understand the different kinds of drilling, the basic equipment used, and what to expect in the industry. It tackles the different kinds of mining sites and drilling methods. It serves as a guide on how you can break into the system, get your dream job, and work your way to become a driller.

Thanks for purchasing this book. I hope you enjoy it!

Chapter 1 – How to Become a Drillers Offsider

<u>What's a drillers offsider?</u>

A driller's offsider's primary role is to assist the driller with their main duties beginning with moving the rig from a set up to the next. As an offsider, you will get orders from the driller and act according to their instructions.

This is an entry-level job for people who aim to become a qualified driller. The tasks you will do will give you substantial experience when pursuing other careers in the drilling industry.

<u>Here are the typical requirements needed for the role of a drillers offsider:</u>

- You have to be healthy and physically fit.

- You must be ready for the physical demands of the job.

- You have to show eagerness in doing hands-on work and in learning new skills.

- You have to observe safety all the time. You must possess a mechanical aptitude.

- It's beneficial to have Cert II or III in Drilling Operations.

- Your driver's license must be without any HR restrictions.

- You have to pass alcohol, drug, and pre-employment medical tests.

- You must be able to work despite extreme weather conditions. You have to be ready for action and must observe punctuality all the time.

- Other companies require certificates on intermediate first-aid and MARCSTA (Mining and Resource Contractors Safety Training Association).

- It's going to be an advantage if you have a rural and heavy laboring background.

How to Become a Drillers Offsider?

As a drillers offsider, you will help move, set up, and operate the drilling rigs. You will also assist in setting up and moving the secondary equipment used in drilling holes for gas or oil production and exploration or mineral exploration.

You need to learn how to use the drill rig and secondary equipment, including water hoses and lines, diesel tanks, and mud shakers, and keep them in good condition. Part of your role aside from getting orders from the driller is collecting core samples, cleaning the rig, tubing, and load casing. If the job requires experience, you will need to obtain Certificate II in Drilling (Mining and Exploration, a course that takes 12 days.

The job requires long hours of work typically done in remote locations. You may be required to work for two weeks and take the next one week off. The job is in the resource industry, including surface coal mining and gas and oil production and exploration.

To make it easier for you to land a job in a drilling company, you must acquire loader/telehandler competency and a HR license.

This job is only a starting point and is necessary for gaining experience. From here, you can move up the ladder depending on what you want to pursue. You may want to get employed in a large-scale company, start your own drilling business, and many more.

<u>As a drillers offsider, you will be given the following tasks and duties:</u>

- Maintain and clean campsites, drill, and equipment

- Perform minor repairs and maintenance tasks, such as cleaning and lubrication

- Operate water and air pumps, shakers and mud pumps, and other equipment

- Clean drainage point and mud pits

- Mix fluids used in drilling and test them

- Help in getting core samples

- Help the driller in operations

Most drilling companies require their drillers offsiders to be over 18 years old before you could work for them. You must be keen on recording details and have good organizational skills. You must also be able to understand and carry out instructions in detail.

The job is crucial, and mistakes are risky. You need to focus whenever on duty and be ready to help and cooperate as a team member.

What You Need to Know Before Pursuing a Career in Drilling

A FIFO job makes good money, and you don't have to worry about your food or rent. FIFO in the mining industry means fly-in fly-out. It may sound lucrative, but this kind of lifestyle doesn't fit everyone.

The workload varies on many factors. You can be required to work 8/6 or work for eight days and take the next six days off, 1/7, 9/5, 14/14, and many more, depending on the project.

Advantages

- You get exposed to different employees from the same company and sometimes from other companies as well. This means that you will learn about the other roles you can pursue in the industry.

- It's easier to develop a rapport and make friends with the people you're working with since you are working together and stay in the same place while the project is ongoing.

- You'd get hand-on to many facilities of high standards that many of these sites use. This gives you a good experience and exposure, something you might miss out on if you're only working close to home.

- You will be able to save up faster, especially if you are still single. The company will primarily provide for most of your needs, which means you won't have too many expenses.

- Once your work is done at the end of the day, the only chore you'd have to do is your laundry.

- You can take advantage of your off time and leave entitlements to go on an international trip, or you can also use the time to bond with your family.

- The R&R or rest and relaxation period are quite long, enough to get the needed break to recover your energy before going back to work.

- Unlike other jobs, you are done for the day once you leave the site. You no longer bring home unfinished tasks, which will eat too much of your personal time.

Disadvantages

- You cannot be caught unprepared. The jobs in the FIFO lifestyle aren't forever. You can't expect everything to last as long as you need. You have to save up and have plans on what you will do once the work ends.

- There is a high chance for meals to get repeated often. Since most locations are remote, workers do not get so many choices when it comes to meals. While they are free, you have to get used to eating the same dishes during your stay.

- Getting acquainted with your workmates can be challenging if you are new and working on a large site.

- This lifestyle is not for those who quickly feel constrained by a prisonlike lifestyle. It's like extended camping wherein you cannot go anywhere else while there is work.

- The rosters and hours of work can be draining. It can also take a toll on your health.

- If you are in a relationship, the lifestyle can cause issues due to lack of time and your absence on important occasions. You have to ensure beforehand that your partner understands your work and all that it entails.

- Not many people will understand the lifestyle, how it works, and why you can't always be there for your friends or family when needed.

Are You Up for the Lifestyle?

Ask yourself the following before pursuing a career in mining. It's not all about the money. You have to prepare yourself in all aspects so that you'd be ready physically, emotionally, and mentally before submitting to the FIFO lifestyle:

1. Have you discussed your plans with your family?

They have to know, and they have to agree with the set-up. It is not easy for everyone, especially if you have grown-up kids, to be away from home for two to four weeks straight. It can take a toll on your personal relationships.

Make sure they understand about the job. Unlike an office job wherein they can still get in touch with you while at work, this is not the case for a FIFO lifestyle. More often than not, you'd rarely be able to communicate with them even after work due to exhaustion.

2. Have you acquired the necessary licenses and tickets?

You need an HR license in most surface-drilling jobs. This is the first step to secure a job, even though you will get by with a C class for an Underground Drilling role.

Ensure that the license is clean. You can't be caught with any offense, so always be responsible.

To get your application on top of the pile, it would help if you finish training courses for the other tickets required, such as Working at Heights, 4WD, and First Aid.

3. Are you fit for the job?

Many drilling sites will require a physical form for their workers. The job may pay well, but it is tough. Some sites restrict their workers to a body mass index (BMI) not exceeding 35. This is to ensure that you will stay healthy no matter what the climate condition is. To help your body prepare for the role, you may want to hire a personal trainer and set an appointment with a dietician.

4. Have you worked in a relevant industry before?

Have you lasted at least a year in a labor-intensive and physically demanding industry? Work may include repetitive, physically tiring tasks, such as scaffolding, brick layering, heavy lifting, or a farm-hand. You must have experienced what it's like to work in a team for long hours, and not mind your physical appearance. Drilling is a repetitive task that requires physical strength. This is not something that you may want to try but back out before the project's completion.

5. Do you have a criminal record?

You need to disclose your criminal records – how long have the charges or convictions lasted, and what were you charged with. Having a criminal record is not the end of your drilling journey as long as you are honest about your past. The people in charge of assigning jobs may consider your cases depending on the request of the employers.

It doesn't mean that you won't get a job. It only means that you will be assigned to tasks or departments that do not have anything to do with your past convictions. For example, if you have been convicted for violence, you may not be placed in a team comprised of closely-knit people working in the heat. If you have been charged with theft, they may avoid putting you in a gold mine.

6. Check if you are physically up for the job.

Different sites have varying requirements for their drillers. Due to climate and site conditions, specific sites require their drillers to have a maximum of 35 BMI or body mass index. It would help to prepare by getting a personal trainer and dietician.

There are charter planes that restrict a passenger to a maximum weight of 130 kilos. There is no other way to fly off to a remote site, but through these planes, so the best thing you can do is keep your weight in check.

You will also be required to undergo medicals for pre-employment that typically lasts two to two and a half hours. You will be required to do a fitness test, drug screening, and rigorous testing of your muscles, breathing, eyesight, and hearing.

Make sure that you get in shape before going to an interview as a Driller's Offsider. You will already be judged at this point whether or not you are fit for the job, so it is best to show up in a great form to increase your chances of cinching the spot.

7. Have you done your research about the job and job hunting?

It is essential to know all that you can about the drilling contractor, especially when it is your first try to apply for a drilling job. You can join support groups in online forums and social media sites or ask for advice from your recruiter.

Once the contract is laid out, you have to prepare everything, including the right questions to ask. Make sure that you are aware of the answers to the following before signing:

- Will the company conduct Cert II and Cert III Drilling on-the-job training during your first year on the job?

- Is the job going to be an ongoing casual contract, or do you have any chances to become permanent after probation?

- Will there be set rosters/set swings?

- Will it be exploration-based or site-based? What is included in the site facilities? How's the accommodation going to be like if it is exploration-based? Will you be given internet or phone access/coverage?

- What's the company's record regarding safety?

8. Do you know anything about the job?

Never commit to the job before you know everything it entails. For example, if you aren't fond of caravans, you have to stay away from exploration drilling. On the other hand, it is not good to pursue underground drilling if you are claustrophobic.

Ask your recruiter about the kinds of drilling available, the machinery used, and techniques employed in the available drilling jobs.

9. What is your long-term goal?

There are higher drilling jobs that require experience and certificates. You will be given opportunities to get qualified for these jobs when you get hired by good drilling companies. Aside from on-the-job training, they will train you to be eligible for Cert III Drilling.

It may not be easy to attain, but if your long-term goal is to pursue drilling jobs around the world, you have to be dedicated to doing things right and completing assessments.

These drilling jobs may be lucrative, but you will work hard for the money, literally. This is not an industry for everybody. You have to be fit, strong, and mentally prepared. Mining sites differ in their difficulty levels. You will be required to work no matter what the season is. You will have a set plan and goal for every project you have to complete, no matter what, before taking a break or calling it done.

Chapter 2 – Increasing Your Chances of Finding Drilling Jobs

Once you have set your mind to work in the mines, the next thing you need to know is how to find a job in this field.

There are no set rules, and the process will depend on the requirements set by an operator. You can use the following information as a guide to breaking it into the industry, but you also have to understand that it would not be too easy.

When starting, you will need to conform to drastic changes in your lifestyle, sacrifice your time, and spend money while job hunting. You need to have a plan. It can be a boom and bust industry, so you have to be prepared to get rejected numerous times before finding a "gold mine."

The competition is tough, especially when you have limited skills. You have to plan how to make yourself stand out and find the right opportunities. Ensure your health while looking for jobs. You will feel drained at times but keep that motivation to get going no matter the outcome.

Where Do You Want to Go?

Before taking any steps further, you have to ask yourself the question - where do I want to go? You will use the answer as motivation, especially at times when you encounter rejections. This way, you will not get easily disheartened, and you will keep trying until you get in.

Your answer to the question will give you a path. It will pick you up when things got rough. From this point, you can work on improving your skills by gaining experience and qualifications.

It will help to ponder on the answers to the questionnaire below. Think hard about your answers. They will help you become more prepared for the rough bumps and successes in this industry where you want to get in.

Questions about Lifestyle

The following questions will help you decide the lifestyle or roster you are willing to have as part of the job:

1. Is your house near large-scale construction or mining work?

If yes, you may want to begin searching for jobs. You never know, but the employers may be scouting for locals for some tasks. This makes looking for additional hands quicker on their part and the total labor cost cheaper.

If not, you have to keep on looking for related jobs somewhere else. This means that you will be relocated once hired. You must also spend time away from home while job hunting and spend more money in the process.

2. How far are you willing to relocate to get the job?

If you don't live near any drilling, mining, or construction sites, you have to decide whether or not you are willing to relocate somewhere else to make it easier for you to find jobs.

You have to set your expectations, though; relocating doesn't guarantee you anything. It only places you to an advantage of becoming a local, which will increase your chances of getting hired by recruiters who favor hiring someone from the community where the site is.

It's not a wise idea to hurriedly pack-up and sells your house. Do your research first about the place where you intend to relocate. Visit property listings, and talk to a couple of local real estate agents to check the best deals you can get.

3. If you are not willing to relocate your roots, are you open to embracing DIDO (drive-in drive-out) or FIFO (fly-in-fly-out) work setting after landing a job?

If you are affirmative about the set-up, you have to beef up for the stiff competition you'll be in. Many of those who want a job in drilling or mining prefer a FIFO setting. The jobs may be more difficult to acquire if you don't have contacts, experiences, and skills.

Here are some of the vital things you must know about the rosters and conditions in a DIDO and FIFO job opportunities:

- Mining and onshore drilling – The general rule for FIFO rosters for mining is several days (7 to 14) of continuous work and longer days off (4 to 14). The number of days at work and days off vary depending on the section and the site you're working for. The set-up is considered family-friendly because you get to spend time with your loved ones for a longer period after working non-stop for several days.

- Offshore drilling – The FIFO rosters, in this case, have longer working days and breaks depending on your rig. For example, you have two weeks of working days and two weeks of break or four weeks of working days and four weeks of break. It can be tough to land jobs in offshore drilling unless you have a beefed-up resume or you know someone who can recommend you for the job.

- FIFO for Construction – As a general rule in construction, work days for FIFO rosters are longer. For example, you will work four or three weeks non-stop and have a week off or work for five weeks and take two weeks off. The schedule may be grueling, but it also means getting paid more. It is also possible to be given a pajama day while on-site, which means you can have a break for one or two days and rest in camp. This set-up often happens on longer rosters to give their men a brief period to recharge before getting back to work.

- DIDO for Construction – The general rule, in this case, is 10 days to 4 weeks on and 4 days to 1 week off.

Questions about Career Change

1. Have you experienced working in any blue-collar industry?

It's a significant advantage if you know the drill of how things work and what's expected of you in a blue-collar job. Your potential employer will see you as someone who knows what the work entails or how you can be trusted to do the job even when left without supervision for a time.

Those who have no experience in the blue-collar industry will be tagged as "green skin." You'd have to start from the bottom once hired. This will teach you the skills and demeanor needed to last on the job. Your efficiency and speed will determine your progress in learning new skills.

Suppose you have experience in any blue-collar jobs but would like to try a different industry. In that case, you may want first to try applying to small to medium-scale contracting companies that work for the owner of the industry you are eyeing, such as power stations, refinery, or mining. Aside from gaining more experience, you have to use your time to know more about the industry – its ins and outs.

For newbies without experience, working for a contractor will make it easier for you to learn the required skills without feeling the stiff competition in the industry. They can adjust your working conditions and negotiations depending on your performance.

2. If you can't find a job as a drillers offsider at once, are you willing to try other jobs that will give you the experience you need?

Experience – this is the word you will often hear when scouting for any drilling jobs. You may sometimes end up wondering how you'd get the experience if no one would take a chance on you. If not a drillers offsider, you may want to try applying for any of the following jobs. The experience you will get from them can help boost your resume.

- Machine operator. While related jobs require other roles, such as maintenance, service, and repair, you will spend most of your time operating a machine. Some samples include crane operator and roller operator.

  As a crane operator, your primary role will be to set up the crane. The other minor roles include setting up the site, doing pre-start checks, demobilizing the machine after lifting, and stabilizing the crane. A roller operator deals with the machine's pre-start and operates it to make the ground surface compact.

- Working with your hands. Some samples of the jobs that fall in this category include fixed plant operators, tradespersons, skilled laborers, and laborers.

  Fixed plant operators usually work in heavy industries, such as mining and energy. They are responsible for controlling their assigned industrial plant functions. If assigned to commissioning and maintenance teams, it is possible to get tasked with jobs, such as maintenance and minor repairs.

  On the other hand, tradespersons, skilled laborers, and laborers can work in various industries. The jobs included deal more with fitting and installing, building, and maintaining.

3. Are you willing to work as a machine operator?

It is ideal to learn how to operate big machines if you want to become a drillers offsider. Remember that the tasks may vary, even using similar machines depending on the industry you are in. Specific industries will require you to have a keen mindset all the time; others need speed; some tasks need a perfect hand and eye coordination, while there are also jobs that will require you to perform monotonous tasks.

Here are some of the common samples of machine-operating jobs you can try to gain experience and move a step closer to your goal of becoming a drillers offsider:

- Underground operators. They typically work in mining sites underground, have a family-friendly schedule, and are paid well. To get the job, you may want to start as a Nipper or be asked to do when told and fetch things for the other workers.

  You will need to pass a theory exam on your first try in applying for the job, which will test your competency. Once you begin working, your competency will be based on your speed of catching up and learning the skills and how comfortable you are when handling a machine.

- Above-ground mobile plant operators. These operators typically get assigned to stockpiling operations, warehouses, surface mining, quarries, and civil construction. Before getting signed off, you will need to pass a theory exam to gauge your competency and gain experience.

  If you want to operate mining machinery but still haven't found a job, you can apply to civil construction and use this as your stepping stone. What machine would you like to try? It depends on your skills and preference. For example, operating a roller often feels monotonous since you will be driving back and forth to make the ground compact. If you don't want to be stuck in such a job, your better option is to operate a grader.

The job needs full awareness to get trimming and angles right.

- Production drillers/gas and oil exploration. The jobs are typically remote with FIFO or DIDO shift settings. This is a good stepping stone to break into offshore drilling. To get into it, you have to undergo on-the-job training and pass theory exams. Some of the machines you can try to operate in these jobs include telehandlers, front-end loaders, cranes, and drill rigs.

4. Do you want to try jobs that require working with your hands?

Even when you are more comfortable working with your hands, you still have to show skills depending on your job. Some jobs require consistent awareness about others and yourself; some jobs need you to have a greater sense of critical thinking, while other jobs require their workers to have a mechanical mindset.

Most jobs that require working with hands include being tradesmen, skilled laborers, unskilled laborers, and fixed plant operators.

Tradesperson

If you are after a higher pay, prioritize jobs at trades than being unskilled or skilled laborers. You need to finish an apprenticeship before you can become a tradesperson. The duration of the internship will depend on the job, but it usually takes five years. It includes the completion of trade competencies at a TAFE college. Take note that tradies will need to hone greater awareness, more skills to work using their hands, and a higher level of technical thinking than what's required with both skilled and unskilled laborers.

Skilled laborers

They are more in demand and get higher pay than unskilled laborers. The training courses required are also not that rigorous and only take a week or less to complete. Getting experience, though, just like in any job, takes longer. These jobs need reasonable levels of ability to use their hands at work, technical thinking, and awareness.

Laborers

They are usually assigned more on the manual than technical tasks. They are given a trade assistant's role in both construction and mining sites and assigned to clean the worksite. The jobs in this category do not require courses to be completed. You only need to have skills in working with your hands, common sense, and readiness to follow instructions.

Fixed plant operators

Their primary role is to ensure safe control and operation of a specific plant's function. They typically work in industries such as mining, heavy, infrastructure, and energy. They work in family-friendly shifts and get paid well. Most of them undergo onsite training typically shouldered by the company to achieve competencies needed in the industrial plant they are in. To get hired for this job, you will need a reasonable ability to use your hands at work, a high level of awareness, and a high level of technical thinking.

__5. While drillers offsiders usually work at mining sites, you need to gain experience to make it easier for you to land jobs in your chosen industry. What other industries are you willing to try your luck on?__

Mining

The mining industry is divided into three types – underground hard rock, underground coal, and open cut. Its purpose to dig mineral ore from the ground. Underground mining techniques are often applied when the mineral deposit is situated beneath the earth's surface. Many coal mines transfer coal to a wash plant facility before selling it to market. Other minerals, such as gold, goes through a leaching process in a separation facility after getting dug to extract gold from the rock.

Many mine sites are found in remote places, so you have to be prepared to agree on a FIFO setup or get relocated if you are serious about getting in. Applying for jobs at mine sites is challenging, so it's best to set your expectations and have other plans to earn while waiting.

Energy

The industry is composed of many functions and energies. They include distribution, refining, manufacturing, oil, and gas fuel extraction, and the sale and production of energy. The workers' roles depend on the project or site, but they are generally similar to heavy industry and mining or something in between. For example, the roles of those involved in oil and gas production and exploration are more similar to those who work at mining sites, and they are also assigned to remote locations. In terms of salary, most of them get something similar to heavy and mining industries. It will likely increase when you apply for offshore positions.

Heavy industry

This industry is considered as the second in line next to a mining site. It's a high-cost industry that requires hi-tech facilities used in processing material, product, or commodity into something that can be transported and used.

The requirement for rosters depends on the company and the product they are processing. The pay is good, but the work schedule depends on the demand for the product. You could be working for 12 hours per day without a day off when production is hectic, or 8 hours per day with two rest days.

Domestic

The industry is similar and, at times, a cross-over, with commercial, including the hours of work and pay. The pay scale ranges from low to middle, and you will be working for 8 to 10 hours per day for 5 days a week. You will be working on people's properties as the industry is involved in the service and building of dwellings, landscaping yards, pools, houses, sheds, and more.

Infrastructure

The industry is comprised of roads, airports, waste treatment, water supply, tunnels, and bridges. It is all about facilities, services, and structures intended to enhance and sustain societies' living conditions. It's a local industry, usually owned by the government or public sector, so the pay is not lucrative. The good thing is since it is local, you'll be able to manage your time and expenses wisely. It also enables you to gain essential experience you can use in applying for other jobs.

Commercial

The jobs entail constructing new buildings and service, maintenance, and repair of buildings or equipment. The industry is comprised of businesses that handle selling and buying of products on a large-scale basis. The pay is from lower to middle, and you will likely be required to work 8 to 10 hours per day for 5 days a week.

Agriculture

It involves the cultivation of foods and animals, farm machinery, transportation, and irrigation. The industry is comprised of the cultivation of crops, plants, livestock, and other products. The work hours are longer. Many of those who get lured to the industry do this for relaxation and to get a high level of satisfaction. You can also try the industry if you want to gain experience in operating large farming machinery.

6. *What types of work are you willing to try?*

There are no shortcuts to any kinds of jobs. In trying out various jobs while waiting to get into a drillers offsider opportunity, take this opportunity to hone various skills. You can use the experience to make your resume look more appealing.

Exploration, blasting, and drilling

This work set is the closest one to what you will perform as a drillers offsider. They are usually done in the oil and gas, energy, and mining sectors. You can work in this field as an oil and gas driller, mobile plant operator, skilled laborer, or tradesperson.

Tradies are tasked to work between the drill rigs used in ensuring safe operations of all equipment, including hydraulics, pumps, vibrators, leads, plugs, lighting, power distribution, and diesel generators. When a malfunction happens, the equipment is brought to Hazardous Area Code for faultfinding and repair.

The skilled laborers assigned on drill rigs are typically tasked as doggers and riggers. They can be promoted upon showing good skills as drillers or derrickmen.

Mobile plant operators set up the needed equipment and prepare the drill site. They set up heavy equipment, including rollers, excavators, water cart trucks, HC truck operators, and graders. They also make sure that the drill site is ready for cleaning, pit construction, or leveling. They hand over the site for the drilling process to start. At this point, operators use cranes to install and relocate the equipment where they are needed.

Telehandlers or front-end loaders handle tubing or load casing of the drill rig to be used at the site. Through the use of water cart trucks, the top part of the hole is flushed with water.

The drilling crew is assigned to setting up and operating the drill rig. They also pull the pieces apart and take them off the site once the well is done. The crew's roles depend on their position, from being a roustabout to a senior driller. Some samples of the work required from them include earth core sampling, downhole drill position, depth, fire watch, cleaning, maintenance, safety shut off of the well, and controlling permits for safety purposes.

Drillers in mining come in two types – grade control and blast hole.

Grade control is tasked with tonnage or grading and fine-tuning the ore boundaries. This will make it easier for engineers to assess the location and depths of the blasting coordinates.

Blast hole drillers charge an explosive shot to the drill according to the depth of the hole. The setup is used to blast until the rock is cleared from the mining's ore body deposit. The shot firer ensures that safe working practices are followed by the MMU operator and crew and takes care of loading and detonation. Both MMU operators and shot firers are typically assigned at day shifts, while blast hole drillers work around the clock; some work at day shift and others at night.

These workers went through emergency training in responding to injuries, environmental problems, and fire. The work location is typically remote, and work is generally up to 12 hours per day.

Operations/process/production

You will typically find this kind of work in oil and gas, energy, heavy industry, and mining. They work as dragline operators, shovel operators, water cart operators, grade operators, dozer operators, and haul truck drivers in mining sites. They are also given tasks related to mineral movement and bulk earth movement. The role is to obtain the mineral, ore, or product from the earth and transfer them to a processing plant.

In other sectors, such as control room, fixed plant, oil and gas, energy, and heavy industry, the tasks mainly include control processes and monitoring of the plant. If you are assigned the job, you have to safely operate the plant without malfunctions.

In all industries, the team assigned with operations works closely with the maintenance trades team. This is a good exposure since you will get extensive knowledge about electricity and mechanisms. Daily tasks are often comprised of responding to injuries, environmental and fire emergencies, equipment repair, lubricating, cleaning, and collecting and analyzing samples. They will train you on how to run and shut down the plant in times of emergencies and what to do to maintain or repair malfunctioning equipment.

Operators can also be tasked with monitoring and issuing isolation permits, permits to work for all trades, and confined space entry permits. Safety is the main focus at this point, and monitoring common work hazards, including working from heights, pressure, ergonomics, mechanical, chemical, noise, and temperature. The rosters are generally family-friendly, with work hours per day ranging from 8 to 12.

Shutdowns

Equipment, site, or plant has a section called a shutdown that refers to jobs required to turn off and remove items from service to undergo upgrades, new installations, and maintenance. The jobs involved are given to skilled workers and a small section of mobile plant operators, fixed plant operators, tradies, and skilled laborers.

Skilled laborers are typically given tasks as doggers, riggers, and scaffolders. Tradespersons are tasked with maintenance, faultfinding, repairing plant equipment, and installing new machinery when needed while the plant is online. They work together with operators in testing that all equipment is ready and safe to use. The operators isolate equipment and ensure the site is safe for the teams to work. They also return the equipment, site, or plant to service once fixed.

You can also find work at this section as a skid steer loader and trucks, cranes, EWP, or forklift operator. The shifts and hours of work will depend on the duration of shutdown and the plant's size. Usually, you have to work for 6 days straight for 10 to 12 hours and take a day off. This will change once you have completed your work's scope in the section you are working on. This job entails a high level of hazards due to the volume of workers in a closed space. Workers and management must coordinate closely with each other to maintain productivity and ensure safety in the workplace.

Maintenance

You will find related jobs in many industries and opt to work as a mobile plant operator, tradies, skilled laborer, and laborer.

As a laborer, you will be assigned manual tasks, cleaning the site, and assistance. If hired as a skilled laborer, you will be handed tasks related to your skills, such as tire fitter, sandblaster, scaffolder, dogger, or rigger.

Tradespersons will be given specialty work in maintenance, repair, fitting, and faultfinding of equipment. Specific sites may need other workers, such as electricians and diesel fitters. For mobile plant operators, you can land jobs in this sector, including HC and HR truck driver, elevated work platform operator, forklift operator, skid steer loader, and crane operator.

The pay in this sector is generally fair, but it still depends on the industry and the company that hired you. Working hours depend on the workload. Normally, you will work for 5 days for 8 to 12 hours per day and have 2 days off.

Construction

Construction work is divided into two categories with tasks that intertwine – buildings/refineries/constructing plants and civil construction. Civil construction is a good stepping stone if you want to get promoted to the other category.

In buildings/refineries/constructing plants, many jobs require mobile plant operators, tradies, skilled laborers, and laborers. Laborers handle trade assisting, cleaning, and other tasks that do not require technical skills. Skilled laborers work as scaffolders, riggers, and doggers. You can also work on the specific job where your skills fit or be asked to work as a trade assistant if needed. You can also apply for day-to-day tasks performed by mobile plant operators, such as excavator operator, truck driver, skid steer loader operator, EWP operator, forklift operator, or crane driver.

Workers in many construction companies work in remote locations with accommodation. The rosters and shifts vary. It can be 4 weeks of continuous work with 1 week off, or 6 days of work and 1 day off. Hours of work have been set to 10 to 12 hours per day in accordance with the fatigue management and risk management implemented by companies. It is better if you will find local construction jobs so that you can rest at home after each day at work.

The construction industry pays well. It is also a good way to learn many skills you can use in applying for jobs at drilling sites. It is important to note that those involved in construction have the highest rate of relationship breakups and suicide among all blue-collar workers. It is easy to get trapped in the job while missing out on your priorities, including your family and loved ones.

As a worker in the industry, you have to keep alert and coordinate with other workers and management. The degree of hazards is high, so you need to be aware of the things and people around you all the time while at work.

Civil construction, on the other hand, entails many types of jobs, except offshore work. The occupations needed in this sector are usually the opposite of the ones required in buildings/refineries/constructing plants. It requires fewer tradies and skilled laborers and more mobile plant operators.

Laborers work on physical tasks, such as using handheld equipment, digging, and spotting. Tradies work on minimal needs for faultfinding, maintenance, and repair or plant equipment.

The sector requires a wide range of mobile plant operators, including excavators, water cart trucks, dump trucks, rollers, scrapers, graders, and dozers. Tasks include leveling the ground, construction of dams, trenching, compacting, and grading the ground.

Working hours depend on the company and project you're working on, ranging from 10 to 12 hours per day. The shifts can be 3 or 4 weeks of continuous work and a week off or 5-week workdays and 2 weeks off.

Your Stepping Stone to Become a Drillers Offsider

After listing your answers to the questions above, it will be easier to plan out your next steps to make it easier for you to land jobs as a drillers offsider. Instead of getting rejected multiple times due to lack of experience, you can use the waiting time to gain experience from other related industries and jobs.

How do you get into these related jobs? Here are the steps to follow once you have decided what other careers to pursue to gain work skills and experience to help you reach your end goal, which is to become a drillers offsider, easier and faster.

<u>1. Study your options.</u>

Search for the available jobs at listings and online. List out the ones that interest you but don't apply yet. Make sure that you have the following qualifications:

- Can pass an alcohol and drug test

- Willing to put effort and time, and shell out some cash during the job hunting process

- You have seen many listings in your preferred locations and options

- Willing to adapt to the FIFO or DIDO work setting and relocate is needed

If you are still not ready, start getting fit and enroll in courses that will boost your qualifications and confidence in looking for jobs.

2. Prepare

Go through the requirements of the jobs you intend to apply to. You have to prepare yourself to fit most of the requirements. This will make it easier for you to sell yourself during the job-hunting process, and more employers will get interested in what you have to offer.

Research. You have to know everything you can about the job positions, companies, people, projects, sites – any other useful facts you can use during job interviews.

3. Let people know about your interest in applying to certain jobs

You have to send out feelers. If you know someone in related industries, ask for help. It is a good time to use your connections to get things moving faster. It is not a job you'd ask, but instead, you will focus on letting people and companies know about your intention. You can also ask questions to get more familiar with the companies or what the jobs entail.

You can also try calling potential employers to ask questions to the human resources personnel. You are not applying for a job yet. You are only after more information about what they are looking for when hiring people. This is also your way of building connections. Show your intent and be enthusiastic about it. You can tell them that you would like to work for them in the future, but you need to ensure that you are fit and qualified. Make sure that you list down all the information you have gathered on the phone, including the name of the person you've spoken to and the company's name.

Another good way of learning insider information about the companies and jobs you're interested in is approaching unions. Not all unions fit the controversial connotations given to them by the media. Most of the union officials care about their members and ensure their protection. This is why they are updated about the local companies in need of people, companies on the verge of downsizing, and their owners' reputations. You will gain many hints in talking to union leaders and members.

You only need the information, but it is still not time to join them. You must first be able to penetrate the workforce and try living that life before deciding whether you will join unions or not. These groups know many practical details about all kinds of industries, especially heavy industry, energy, and mining.

You can search online for the list of union groups near you. List down the contact details of the people you can get in touch with and reach out as soon as you can.

4. Continue learning while gaining experience

Gather everything you will need in looking for jobs. Prepare your interview clothes, budget, and most especially, yourself. To make it easier for you to sell yourself, you have to update your resume based on the things you've learned in your research.

Do not despair if you don't have any experience. This is why you are looking for jobs – you are building up your resume until you are qualified to become a drillers offsider. For now, you can start small but make sure that you give your best no matter what that job is. Your goal is to learn as many skills as possible, get to know people and get closer to your dream job.

You already know what most employers are looking for, so consider them when making changes to your resume and practicing your answers to job interviews.

<u>5. Check that your resume is complete</u>

Before you begin sending out your resume to possible employers, go over every detail and ensure it's flawless – no spelling or grammar mistakes. Remember that you'll be in a tough competition, and you would not want your resume to get ignored when the first thing the HR personnel sees in your resume is an error.

- The resume must capture whoever would read it in 10 seconds upon scanning the content. Imagine yourself in their position and set a standard for the kind of resume that would catch your interest.

  Remember to write the names of the people who interviewed and assisted you during the application process. This way, you can add a personal touch when you make your follow-up phone calls to get updated about your application's status.

- If you leave the resume to the company's receptionist or only mail it, address it directly to the HR staff responsible for recruiting people for the job you are applying for. You can ask the receptionist or call the company regarding the matter. Make sure that you politely ask since they may not readily give this kind of information to anybody.

- In the work experience section, include the details that may give your resume a boost and not the other way around. If you held several positions over a short period, come up with a sound explanation of why. Many companies frown upon those people who "jump ship" often. Unless you explain using the right words, it will appear to the recruiter that you easily get bored with your job or get lured with other jobs even after giving your commitment to one company. Be specific in this section, and never assume that the HR person would read between the lines when going through your resume.

- Check that your qualifications, licenses, or tickets are updated. Scan your tickets in color and make sure they are not expired. They need these items to hire you. You can't expect the HR personnel to chase after you to get the updated documents. This negligence can cause you to snatch the job.

- Make sure that the people you included in the reference list know you and will remember you when a company representative calls them. You must also inform them that you have included them on the list to avoid getting surprised upon receiving a call. Include their full name, position title, and their email address, and/or phone number.

<u>6. Try and try until you nail it</u>

You are still trying to find your roots in the industry and gain as much experience as possible to make it easier for you to become a drillers offsider. Even if this is not your dream job, you have to give your best and make a good impression each time you are given a chance for an interview.

Never lose hope each time you get a rejection, but learn from what you think went wrong. This will help you improve the way you carry and "sell" yourself to the interviewers the next time you get a call.

Once you are given a chance, treat the job as if it is your dream job. Work hard while honing your skills. Be patient with the process. It may take time before you get used to the job and the workplace, but everything will get easier over time. Promotions will come to those who deserve them, so work each day to speed up the process of climbing up the ladder.

When you reach the point that you want to give up, think hard about the decision first. You've already gone far and did too much. Go to the questionnaire and start from the top. Are you ready to go job hunting all over again? Do so only if you think that you've gained enough experience and skills from the job.

Chapter 3 – A Day in a Life of a Drillers Offsider

The job is hard, dirty, and you can't quit working when it is too hot or too cold. Are you up for the challenge of becoming a drillers offsider?

Here's an example of a day in the life of Rex, an assistant driller with more than ten years of experience working. He has been working as a drillers offsider for three years on a site found in Alberta, Canada. It's a camp job that requires 20 working days and ten days off.

Start of the day:

Rex wakes up at the sound of his alarm at 5:30 in the morning. Before the crew truck comes to him and his team to work, he gets ready, eats breakfast, and drinks coffee.

Rex, along with the team, gets changed once at the site and meets the rest of the team at the doghouse.

A doghouse on a drilling rig pertains to the structure found beside the rig floor. It has a computer system that monitors and records the activity on site. This is where the members meet at the start of the day and conduct safety meetings.

It's a steel-sided room that serves many purposes aside from being a meeting place and communications center. It is also used as a lunchroom, coffee room, office, and tool shed.

Meetings:

The crew conducts hand-over or change-over meetings to get briefed about the duties from the previous shift. They are told crucial information about the tasks ahead - how the rig is operating, what happened during the night, and what they need to accomplish.

When the meeting is done, the night crew leaves to rest, while Rex, along with his team, proceeds to have safety meetings.

They plan out their day and the job scopes, and they conduct job safety analysis (JSA) and safety meetings. Once done, the team is cleared to get on with their duties.

<u>What Rex Needs to Do:</u>

As a drillers offsider, Rex's responsibilities include the following:

- Ensure the safety meetings are conducted before work starts in the morning

- Ensure daily operations run smoothly and as planned

- Check to see the other crew members are carrying on with their duties and responsibilities on the rig

- Assist the driller whenever needed

Other Tasks

Rex handles the controls as the driller manages the books. They usually deal with the repairs and maintenance, which cannot be done when drilling while they are tripping.

In drilling, everything has to be secured and safe. Rex checks the tasks done by the new and inexperienced people on the team to ensure security before proceeding with related jobs.

After a 12-hour shift, Rex, along with the team, go back to what they call their "home," the camp. It provides them with lodging, meals, weight room, and entertainment.

With this kind of environment, you need to develop a fast rapport with your team. You will not only be working with them, but you will be living and do most things with them. They will be your second family while you are away from home.

Many newbies fear that it might get too cold while working. For the likes of Rex, he has experienced all kinds of weather in extremities. Work continues despite the weather condition.

You will be given the proper gear and clothes to proceed working whatever the weather is.

Time to Relax

After the long days spent at the site, you will have ten days or more vacation or days off from work. The likes of Rex would spend this duration with his loved ones. He would travel and pursue activities he had always wanted to do, such as horseback riding or mountain climbing. He would also use the time on games and leisure he enjoys, such as swimming, biking, playing golf, and many more.

You only have to make sure that you don't injure yourself as you enjoy. Use the time to recharge and do the things you are deprived of while at the camp. While enjoying, keep in mind that you have responsibilities to go back to after your break.

What People Think Drillers Offsiders Do

Have you searched online discussions about how a typical day of a driller's offsider looks like? Here are the common answers you will likely be given when you pose the question on the Web. The good thing about the answers is that many of them came from those who have experienced the job:

"You will handle the drag hoses and drill rods."

"You need to be ready to do tasks, such as handling the core boxes and shovel cuttings, pull or install submersible pumps, change tires, spool winch cables, drive the water buggy, aid in mechanical repairs, plug the boreholes, and mix the mud."

"As you get by, you may be required to drive trucks and operate the drill."

"Prepare to shake three meters of a solid rock sample until it's out of a tube. You can only imagine how heavy this is."

"If you happen to be on a diamond drill rig, prepare to couple and uncouple drill rods with Stillson wrenches that weigh 10 kilos. You will retrieve 100-meter drill rods from the holes to change the drill bit before putting them back where you got them."

"RC is more difficult than diamond drilling. The drill bits weigh around 60 kilos. You need to change the rods connected to a hydraulic arm."

"For every meter drilled at the site, it is your responsibility to collect samples and put them in bags. You will lay the bags in line in consecutive order. This may sound like an easy task, but wait until you get into your 20th or 30th bag. Each bag contains around 20 kilos of mud. You are running back and forth to lay the bag, get the next one and replace it before running again."

"The job is tough, but it becomes tougher when they assign you in a remote location along with people you may not like and not like you either."

"Novices usually lose a lot of weight during the first weeks in the job, but they develop good muscles, especially in the arms."

"The job is physically and mentally tiring. It's a physical job, so you have to eat enough to keep your body fueled."

"Many modern rigs used at sites include machines capable of picking up the rods. You will only be responsible for swinging the rods into place."

"Diamond drilling is more exciting but is also more physically demanding than RC. Many things are happening, and you will learn a lot from your tasks."

How to Step Up as a Driller?

If you are after a lucrative job despite the lack of a college degree, your best option is to become an offshore driller. The position has consistently ranked at various business publications, including Yahoo and Forbes, as one of the jobs that pay far above average even for people who did not finish college.

The job is physically demanding, and as described by those who have gone the path, it is more dangerous than working in the International Space Station or a nuclear submarine. It is a great advantage if you have a long experience as a drillers offsider. You'd be familiar with the stress and loneliness that come with the workload, shifting schedules, and living conditions.

It may be an unforgiving job, but it is highly rewarding. You need to prepare harder if this is the path you've chosen to take.

Here's a look at how you can become an offshore driller, including the steps you need to make before getting a job as a drillers offsider:

1. Finish high school

It is important to finish high school or earn a GED before applying to jobs in the drilling industry with the goal of becoming a driller in the future. More than intelligence, your high school diploma is proof you are responsible. This will make a good impression on your potential employers.

2. Get experience by taking an apprenticeship on a land rig

Even when you have connections to skip this step, it will help if you undergo apprenticeship training for a year or two. This will help you become more familiar with the industry and the work involved. It will also help you build friendships and learn how to work with a team.

3. Look for roustabouts and sign in

You can skip step 2 after graduating from high school and sign on instead as a roustabout. The edge of those who did not skip apprenticeship is that they are more prepared. Even if they will do almost the same tasks as a roustabout – clean stuff, haul heavy equipment, paint the deck; they are more ready for the tough work-life ahead. The pay is good, with a starting monthly salary of around $50,000, but the pay is commensurate with the hard work required by the job.

4. Aim to get promoted to roughneck

If you want to reach this point, you have to do your apprenticeship and stint as a roustabout right. You need to show people, especially the higher-ups, that you are a team player. Do your job well all the time by giving your best, keep on learning, never be a nuisance, and refrain from complaining.

The work is already stressful as it is, so the least the team needs is a member who keeps on complaining or who often commits mistakes. A year of good performance may land you a promotion to roughneck, or even less if you have shown above-average performance and dedication.

You will still be tasked with hard manual labor as a roughneck, but you will spend more time in the actual drilling process. The tasks include inserting and extracting drills, working with the different tools, and laying down the pipe.

5. Keep on getting promoted

After showing good performance as a roughneck, you can get promoted as a pumpman and then as a derrickman. A pumpman works as an assistant to a derrickman and has more responsibilities than a roughneck. A derrickman helps the drillers regarding the workflow's direction, making the position lean more towards a managerial role. To get to this point, you have to keep a good attitude at work and with the rest of the team.

6. Get promoted as an assistant driller

This is what you have been working on – getting experience and expanding your network to become an assistant or a drillers offsider. Five to ten years of previous work experience is enough to land this gig. You will be working as the driller or rig manager's right-hand man and act as a supervisor to roughnecks to derrickmen.

7. Decide if you are still up to get promoted

The years you've spent at work from the beginning up to this point may have already earned you a good sum of savings and a good life. You've lasted long enough in the industry and know the people and how it works. Many offshore drillers stop at step 6 and choose to retire while they are still capable of enjoying the fruits of their long years of hard labor. You don't have to follow in their footsteps if you intend to become a driller or a rig manager.

If you want to work in the same industry with higher pay but less tasking role, you may want to become a geologist instead of a driller. They get paid similar to drillers but work in a less stressful setting. To become a geologist, you need to go back to college and take an advanced degree in business, engineering, geology.

Chapter 4 – Exploration vs. Underground Drilling

Exploration Drilling

Exploration drilling entails a drill string getting sunk into the ground while injecting a special mud. The process allows samples of gas and fragments of rock brought to the surface. It needs several boreholes drilled at different points to ensure the delineation of potential deposits.

Drilling gives details on whether or not prospects contain gas or oil. These prospects vary in depth - from 100 meters or so up to 6,000 meters. The goal is to reach the depth, so a borehole is grilled in stages, with its diameter gradually decreasing in each drill.

Everything needs to be set up in place before the drilling begins. For one, the derrick that will act as the drill pipes' support needs to be in place. The first drill pipe, which will go through the rock formation, is connected to a drill bit or trepan and punched or pressed onto the rock before the drill heads are spun at a high rotation speed.

As the drill pipe goes deeper underneath, the previous pipe is screwed with a new drill pipe. This will go on until the operators get the right length. All the pipes connected constitute the drill string.

The Drilling Mud

Mud is important in the process as it is continuously injected into the holes as the drilling happens. This mud is carefully prepared by mixing solid clay particles, water, and chemicals to make the mixture stable, standard, and dense. The mud's composition differs depending on the pressure in the reservoirs and the kinds of rock to deal with.

Each operation usually requires a specialist to monitor the mud's properties and change the composition as soon as any problem arises. The mud's density needs constant monitoring. It can't be too light because it can lead to a dangerous blowout. It can also not be too heavy, or it might quickly enter into the reservoirs due to the lower pressure than the borehole's inner area.

Drilling mud is essential for the following reasons:

- It balances the pressure in the reservoirs and the inner part of the borehole. This helps in preventing sudden blowouts of gas, oil, or water from the reservoirs.

- The sides of the borehole become more stable due to the counter-pressure the mud provides.

- It brings the cuttings or rock fragments up to the surface.

- It helps in attacking the rock and flushing out the cutting accumulated at the well's bottom part.

- It helps in cooling down the drilling tool, preventing it from overheating by circulating in the borehole in a continuous process.

What Happens Before Extraction?

Drilling reduces or clears up many uncertainties of the prospect. They include the presence of gas or oil and the volume and type of reserves. The appraisal needs to be performed before extraction, comprised of additional wells. These other wells are important in choosing the best locations for production wells to be used in the future. Drilling several wells at various points makes a higher chance for the deposit to be delineated accurately. During the appraisal state, a decision is formed to develop the deposit or abandon it for good.

The Common Hazards Faced in Exploration Drilling

The activity is generally hazardous, but more so when the drilling is done in remote locations for mineral exploration. The hazards may come from various factors, including the drill rig operation, drill pads, worksites, and camps' preparation.

A code of practice is thereby implemented depending on the location of the drilling for mineral exploration. This helps the operators identify the problems earlier on to prepare for whatever may happen and be always ready. These problems or potential hazard risks are categorized, which include:

- Housekeeping
- Existing workings
- Natural gases
- Remoteness of exploration
- Heavy vehicle movement
- Light vehicle movement
- Extreme weather and bushfires
- Hot work
- Ionizing radiation
- Noise
- Dust
- Fatigue and mental wellbeing
- Working in hot environments
- Falling objects
- Working at height
- Manual tasks

- Electricity

- Dangerous goods and hazardous substances

- Hydraulic systems

- Compressed air systems

- Moving and rotating parts

Underground Drilling

Aggregate producers and equipment manufacturers work together in keeping the mines and machines productive in underground drilling. Producers open underground mines by either inclining to a deposit below-ground, sinking a shaft, or performing horizontal drilling from an adjacent quarry. A suite of mining equipment takes on the job after the floor level is reached when a deposit has been burrowed using different tunneling machines.

A basic mine that uses this kind of drilling has one or more two-boom jumbo drills and at least one single-boom drill. Underground rooms also commonly have auxiliary operating equipment and trucks and aggregate loaders used in conveying material to the surface.

Producers choose the drilling machines for their projects depending on the requirements of the operation. They typically go through the following procedures:

1. Choosing a drill rig

Producers choose drill rigs with hydraulic and mechanical features to maximize production. One particular feature they are after is tramming speed. While all the machines do not move as quickly, their speed and nimbleness are relative. A single mph makes a difference since each minute not spent drilling reduces each shift's total production.

2. Single or two-boom rigs?

The choice lies mostly in the number of open faces to drill for every shift. A pair of single boom drills can work faster on a mine with 7 to 10 open faces, but a two-broom rig will drill more quickly in other cases. It all boils down to the hardness of the rock and the operator's skills.

3. The operator's well-being

In choosing an underground drill rig, the U.S. Mine Safety and Health Administration (MSHA) suggests that the focus must be on safety issues and worker environment. These factors include reducing dust and noise emissions, reducing the physical risks for the operators, and their long-term physical comfort. Many manufacturers of today diligently comply even to the point of exceeding the set standards.

The Common Hazards in Underground Drilling

Hazards and accidents are part of the drilling industry, including underground mining. Here are the top five common threats in this field:

1. Flood

Some flooding in the mines is planned and controlled, but the unintentional ones are disastrous and can even be fatal. The following factors can bring about accidental flooding of the mines:

- Old, improper, or lack of mining infrastructures, such as broken or damaged pipes, broken water mains, and leaks

- Intentional explosions

- Unsafe conditions of the mine

One unforgettable example of a mining accident due to flooding happened on September 15, 2011. It happened at the Gleision Colliery after an accidental blast resulting from an explosive's intentional detonation by seven miners. Four of the miners got trapped underground despite the rescue workers' efforts to get them, and the other three escaped.

The incident led the United Kingdom's Health and Safety Executive (HSE) to issue the HID 4-2011 safety bulletin to focus on Precautions Against Inrushes under Regulations 1979. The regulation was first enacted when seven miners died due to a flooded mine at the Lofthouse Colliery in 1973

2. Fire

Aside from being one of the most challenging, fire and explosives are among the most dangerous and destructive hazards in the industry. It can happen anytime, whether the mine site is abandoned or active. In line with this, the HSE issued the document, "The prevention and control of fire and explosion in mines," and lists out the following as the potential causes of fire in mines underground:

- Flammable materials used by smokers, such as matches, lighters, and cigarettes

- Hot work, such as grinding, welding, and burning

- Compression of gasses or air

- Detonators and explosives

- Earth faults and short circuits on distribution systems and electrical equipment

- Mechanical and electrical equipment and machines; hot surfaces and electrical sparks

- Broken coal in high-risk seams or spontaneous heating of coal

- Hot surfaces, air inlets, exhaust systems, and other hazards coming from internal combustion engines

- Defective bearings causing friction, including wheels and axles, drums, and conveyor idlers

A mine site getting caught on fire can be deadly not only to the people working on site but also to the entire town. In 1962, the whole city of Centralia, Pennsylvania, was evacuated due to a fire in a coal mine. Its exact cause was never determined.

3. Collapse

Here are the common reasons why an underground mine could collapse:

- Methane gets trapped in layers of coal. Coal dust explosions can happen due to intentionally detonated explosives, malfunctioning or improperly used tools, and mechanical errors. All these reasons lead to the secretion of methane, a highly explosive gas. This is what happened in 1962 at the Benxihu Colliery in Benxi, China. Coal dust exploded, and a fire broke out after the release of methane, which killed more than 1,500 miners.

- Use of explosives. Explosive can create a similar effect to an earthquake, which can cause the collapse of mine workings. It can also cause damage to the structure, flooding, and the miners getting trapped. This is the cause of the incident that happened from August to October 2010 when 33 miners got trapped underground in a Chilean mine.

- Pillar or timbering failure. Timbers and pillars are used in mining sites to support the tunnel's face or roof during the lining or excavation process. If not secured, they may collapse and lead to accidents.

- Gas or dust explosion. Explosions caused by coal dust and gasses like methane can damage properties and cause the miners' death or getting trapped.

- Induced seismicity. This usually happens in seismically active regions where mine sites are found, like the Andean region. It may be one of the richest metallic mining zones worldwide, but it is also at a high risk of collapsing.

4. Toxic contaminant

The atmosphere underground is confined and limited. It is easy for contaminants to get trapped, including gasses from the rock strata, fumes and particulates from blasting, diesel fumes, aerosols, and dust. It is essential to keep a healthy level of ventilation underground.

5. Other hazards caused by blasting

- Premature blasting. The problem can be caused by damaged fuses or faulty wiring or due to accidental blasting or carelessness. All pyrotechnical and explosive materials in the muck pile or on the ground can get triggered by mechanical effects caused by mining processes, such as crushing, milling, or digging.

- Explosive fumes. Toxic fumes can be fatal in both underground and surface mining. The common belief that fumes disperse quickly in the open air is not valid. Miners must always prioritize proper ventilation no matter where they are working.

- Fly-rocks. Both underground and surface miners are at risk of suffering injuries caused by flying rocks. They may come from improper handling or when miners work closely to the blast site.

Learning about the Equipment Commonly Used in Drilling Jobs

It is crucial to get familiar with the tools and equipment used in the industry to make it easier for you to learn how to operate them once you are given the task. It is a dangerous industry, so learning is crucial to minimize work-related risks and hazards. You will undergo training on how to use the equipment before your bosses allow you to handle them.

To give you a heads-up, here are the common equipment you'd likely be working with as you progress in various positions in the drilling industry:

1. Blasting tools

Good blast designs are necessary for successful mining operations. Too many explosives and poor work practices can lead to unwanted caving due to damaged rock structures. Blasting tools are used to fracture and break down rocks and other materials and get rid of unwanted material pockets. The tools help in making it easier to get the material of interest by separating it from the waste material. They are used in both open mining and underground operations and are considered one of the most dangerous parts of the job.

Depths and positions have been pre-determined at the blasting site before the unmanned drill rigs are set to drill holes. This will reduce the overburden with the blasting as well as the handling costs of materials. The setup will make it possible to achieve a particular size fraction on a blast face.

After blasting, an excavator handles the recovery of the debris and blasted rocks. The material is transferred to the central conveying system to take it to the surface.

2. Mining drills

All workers ensure proper setup of the mining sites before any work could begin. All the workers need to ensure their safety and the success of each operation. Drills are among the essential pieces of equipment used in underground mining.

The drills help in making holes to reach the underground. Miners also use the drills when working underground to fix the size of the holes used as an entry portal for them.

Mining drills are also utilized in drilling wells in employing one type of mining technology, which is directional drilling.

3. Crushing equipment

There are various kinds of mining crushing equipment used at sites depending on the jobs needed to be done. They are designed to attain a high reduction rate and maximum productivity. The equipment helps break down gravel or hard rock into a size that is easy to transport or place on a conveyor.

This way, the handling of the materials becomes more manageable and cheaper. The run of mine (ROM) material is conveyed to the main crusher in underground mining operations and moved to the crusher using haul trucks in strip mining or opencast operations.

4. Equipment used for online elemental analysis, conveying, and feeding

The feeding device takes the raw material from the excavator transporter and feeds it to the crusher for processing. The material gets screened to attain the proper size fraction, and any oversized item gets back and recirculated to the crusher.

The feeding equipment is usually called Weightfeeders. It controls the feed rate while conveying materials into the crusher. This way, it helps the crusher perform its task properly and efficiently. Conveying and feeding equipment are used in the mining industry to control the flow and move the material within mining and processing operations.

There are instances when materials need to undergo secondary crushing to achieve the right size, in which fraction processing is done through the most applicable methods, such as leaching, floatation, or milling.

Belt scale systems deal with the product loadout by allowing workers to monitor inventory and production output. It also helps in ensuring efficient operation and management at work by providing vital information.

Elemental crossbelt analyzers are utilized in controlling out-of-seam dilution, blending, and facilitate sorting. They provide quality analysis of essential process streams in real-time. An automatic sampling system, which can either be multi-stage or single, can directly take a sample from the materials while on a moving troughed belt conveyor. The system helps increase profits, maintain consistency of blend and reduce material consumption.

5. Earthmovers

The equipment is meant to speed up mining projects and work on large earth-moving tasks. They make the job practical and faster. Earthmovers are used for above-ground mining in carrying loose soil from one spot to the next. A highly-skilled operator maneuvers the machine to push, dig and transport the earth.

Earthmovers are used along with bulldozers, a combination essential in the industry. Earthmovers aid in getting rid of waste material or overburden, which the bulldozers move out to clear the working surface for other heavy equipment, such as excavators and haul trucks.

Chapter 5 – The Different Types of Drilling

Drills are categorized into two: types that produce core samples and the types that make rock chips. The drill mechanisms vary depending on the samples produced, the depth that the drill can achieve, penetration rates, and costs.

Air core drilling

Air core drilling utilizes tungsten drill bits of three-bladed steel to make holes. This inexpensive drilling method is used when it is essential to attain clean and safe removal of sample material.

This is more cost-effective and faster than diamond drilling and rotary air blast drilling. The process flushes cutting samples out of the drill holes through the use of compressed air. As a result, samples are acquired without obvious damage to their surrounding area. Through this, the samples collected can be used for a more effective analysis.

Air core drilling is typically used on the unconsolidated ground with an optimal depth of 300 meters for first-pass exploration drill programs. This is preferred by organizations in need of samples with minimal risk of cross-contamination.

<u>The Pros</u>

Here are some of its advantages as compared to the other kinds of drilling processes:

1. Less risk of cross-contamination. The process results in less sample pollution as it blows compressed air into the inner tube to flush the samples.

2. Reduced costs and a higher level of efficiency. The process allows sample collection in real-time, making it efficient and fast. The lesser time spent in drilling means lower field costs. The rigs used in the process are easier to transport since they are lighter than the rigs used in other drill processes.

3. Safer sample extraction. The process ensures less damage to samples due to its reliance on the injection of compressed air. This advantage is more evident when compared to the samples acquired through blast drilling.

4. Delivers good sample materials. The samples extracted in the process are easier to examine and analyze than the samples acquired through other drilling methods.

5. Doesn't require casting holes

<u>The Cons</u>

The process also has certain setbacks, which include the following:

1. Limited ability to penetrate fresh rocks. This process usually finds it hard to go through a fresh rock, but it can drill through cap rock using a tri-cone roller or hammer.

2. Limited depth. The process is typically limited to 50 to 120 cm depth, but it still depends on several variables.

3. The process can be slower than the other methods. While the process is efficient, the speed of drilling is slower when compared to other drilling forms.

Air Core Drilling Bits

The process can only produce efficient results through the use of good quality air-core drilling bits. A drilling bit of high standard is made from quality materials that can withstand the stress, especially when drilling something valuable as quartz. You can also rely on that this bit will deliver versatility and reliability due to its shell and blade design and improved shock resistance.

On the other hand, using air core drill bits with poor quality will result in a longer drilling process and inefficient result. There will be more chances for thick earth in the clay-like form to block the drill, or worse, it will break in the poor quality kind. This would mean work stoppage and wasted money.

Comparing Air Core and RC Drilling

The equipment used in both processes, RC and air core drilling, is similar. The difference lies in the mechanism involved. They both flush out samples using compressed air.

RC drilling is ideal for harder ground. It adds power to the drill bit using an element of concussive force. As a result, the rock becomes pulverized in the process of drilling. This is also preferred in drilling greater depths.

Air core drilling is preferred on shallow depths and unconsolidated ground.

Sonic or vibratory drilling

This type of drilling sends resonant vibrations of high frequency down to the drill bit. The drill head can also generate the same vibrations. An operator controls the frequencies to make them compatible with the rock or soil geology conditions, typically from 50 to 120-hertz cycles per second.

The vibrational forces are isolated from the rest of the drill rig through an internal spring system. Penetration becomes easy in most geological formations due to the magnified amplitude of the drill bit made possible by the resonance. It results in the soil particles' fluidization at the bit face.

Rotary drilling

This drilling method is adopted to drill oil and water to reasonable depths using sand formation and soft, yielding clay. Aside from being low cost, it is capable of penetrating quickly and generally easy. This method can drill up to 1,600 feet in 36 hours or less in a favorable ground without rock strata and heavy gravel.

The method uses a pipe that rotates through machinery situated on the derrick floor. At its lower end, a drill bit is placed to cut the space allotted for the drill pipe using the same effect and motion as an auger. Through a pump, water gets on the drill pipe and escapes through the bit. As it happens, the cuttings are removed and pushed out of the drill pipe onto the surface. The hole remains open in this case, which allows the drill stem to rotate freely. The muddy water column provides ample pressure to hold up the hole walls until the casing has been done.

Percussion Rotary Air Blast Drilling (RAB)

This drilling method is commonly used in the world of mineral exploration using Down-the-hole. It's a hollow piston-driven kind of drill utilizing a pneumatic reciprocating motion to push the drill bit as deep as possible into a rock. It's made of solid steel and thick tungsten rods with about 20 mm thickness. The rods protrude as buttons from the medium, and these buttons become the bit's cutting face. The cuttings get blown to the surface and lifted through wind or the combination of wind and foam.

Since the cuttings get blown out of the rods, they can acquire contamination from other rocks. This is the reason why TAB can only produce samples of lower quality. This kind of drilling can be applied in engineering, drilling in mines using blasting holes techniques, water bore drilling, and mineral exploration.

If the RAB drilling encounters water once it gets to an extreme depth, the hole outside can be clogged with debris. Reamers or stabilizers are used by attaching them to the string of the drill in order to avoid the holes getting clogged. These stabilizers are big cylindrical items created with sizes that suit the hole size being drilled to a tee. They have tungsten buttons and a collection of rollers at the side, responsible for breaking down and pushing the cuttings upwards.

The method can drill deeper holes when combined with air compressors using high-powered machines. The air pressure causes any water and rock cuttings to be pushed down. This drilling method's efficiency can be affected by different factors, including the drill bit's condition and the weight and density of the rock.

RC or Reverse Circulation Drilling

This method has similarities with another drilling technique – the air core. It drills until the cuttings accumulated in the rods are returned outside. It utilizes a piston with a pneumatic reciprocating drilling mechanism and larger machinery and rigs.

The method is ideal in producing dry small rocks as the rock gets dried in the drill bit due to the large air compressors used. It penetrates better and deeper than air core drilling and RAB, but it is more expensive and slower to use. It is preferred in many mineral exploration projects since it is less costly than the coring done using a diamond drill.

The circulation reverses due to the air blown through the rods, in which the air pressure lifts cuttings and water upward inside the tube in each rod. The cuttings move around in a cyclone until they reach the bottom's opening and gather in a bag intended for the samples.

The most widely used drill bots are the kinds with a diameter of 13 to 20 cm with the bit having circular metal buttons protruding. These buttons are necessary for drilling through abrasive and shale rock. Drilling becomes more relaxed as the buttons get worn out. It can also lead to the rods in the hole getting bogged down, a potential problem since recovering the rods can take hours up to weeks. They are also expensive so losing the rods means more expenses. Most companies try to prevent the problem by re-grinding the drill bits' buttons, making the process faster.

Water is used in this drilling method even though it is powered by wind. It helps make a collar in a new hole, assists in pushing the cuttings upwards, keeps the coolness of the drill bit and reduces the dust. The sand gradually gets closer through the process, helping the sample find it easier to reach the surface. Another product is also utilized occasionally, called the Super-Foam, to push the finest elements to the front and make the hole tidy.

Auger Drilling

This method of drilling is done by driving a helical screw to the ground with rotation. The screw's blade lifts the earth the borehole. For grounds where the holes will find it hard to stay open, such as swamps, hollow stem auger drilling is used. This applies to projects, such as geochemistry reconnaissance tasks in exploring mineral deposits, soil engineering, geotechnical drilling, and environmental drilling.

For projects situated in harder grounds, bucket or solid flight augers are employed, or in some instances, auger drills are used along with mine shafts. In general, this type of drilling method, considered fast and cheap, is restricted to sites with weak, weathered rock and soft and unconsolidated material.

Exploration Diamond Drilling

This drilling method is also known as diamond core drilling. It helps cut a cylinder-shaped core of hard rock through the hollow drill rods attached with an annular diamond-impregnated drill bit. The method utilizes industrial-grade diamonds ranging from fine to the tiniest set in a matrix that varies in hardness.

The rigs need to drill slowly to ensure that the rods and drill bits will last long in good condition since they are quite expensive. Drilling takes place at sites with hard rock at the surface, and it can go at depths from 1200 to 1800 meters. The condition of the ground undergoing the drilling process makes the method slower than RC drilling.

In retrieving core samples, a deep and heavy tube is inserted in the string of the rod. It is filled with water up to the point when it gets locked to the center of the barrel. The latter then slide as the core is drilled and cut. As the core tube is pulled to the surface, its sample moves into the tube until it gets detached from the hole. Workers get the sample obtained from the core and proceed ints cataloging the item. It is then rinsed and measured. Once the sample is clean, A hammer is used to break it into pieces that will fit in the trays intended for the samples. The geologists retrieve the samples after getting cataloged and analyze them to decide if the area is a probable lucrative spot for future mining explorations.

Conclusion

I'd like to thank you and congratulate you for transiting my lines from start to finish.

I hope this book was able to help you understand what to expect in the industry and make it easier for you to pursue your dream of becoming a drillers offsider. It will help if you will start from the bottom and work your way up. This will give you enough experience and skills to perform your job well and to ensure your safety while at work.

The next step is to prepare yourself and update your resume. It may be a challenging road ahead, but with determination and hard work, you will eventually land the job, which you can use as a platform to attain higher successes in the future.

I wish you the best of luck!